GREEN-
COLLAR
CAREERS

LEGALLY GREEN

CAREERS IN ENVIRONMENTAL LAW

By Susan Brophy Down

CRABTREE
Publishing Company
www.crabtreebooks.com

Crabtree Publishing Company

Author: Susan Brophy Down
Publishing plan research and development:
   Sean Charlebois, Reagan Miller
   Crabtree Publishing Company
Editors: Mark Sachner, Molly Aloian
Proofreader: Crystal Sikkens
Editorial director: Kathy Middleton
Photo research: Ruth Owen
Designer: Westgrapix/Tammy West
Production coordinator: Margaret Amy Salter
Prepress technician: Katherine Berti
Print coordinator: Katherine Berti
Production: Kim Richardson
Curriculum adviser: Suzy Gazlay, M.A.

Written, developed, and produced by Water
Buffalo Books

Photographs and reproductions:
Tea Benduhn/Nate Norfolk: page 31
Corbis: Bettmann: page 19 (right); Bettmann: page 23; Mast Irham:
   pages 24–25; page 30 (bottom); Peter Essick: page 32; Julie
   Dermansky: pages 38–39 (main); Julie Dermansky: page 39 (top);
   Michael S. Yamashita: page 50 (right top); Michael S. Yamashita:
   page 50 (right bottom)
Ecoscene: Wayne Lawler: page 8 (top)
Peter Fairley: page 29 (right)
FLPA: Richard Du Toit: pages 6–7 (main); Frans Lanting: pages
   10–11 (main); pages 16–17; Flip Nicklin: page 47 (right)
Getty Images: Kambou Sia: page 30 (top); Simon Maina:
   page 41; page 52; Spencer Platt: page 54; page 55; Adek
   Berry: page 57 (bottom)
Douglas Meiklejohn: page 5 (bottom right)
Tara Sawatsky: page 57 (top)
Science Photo Library: David Nunuck: page 56
Shutterstock: cover; page 1 (top); pages 4–5 (main); page 4 (bottom);
   page 5 (bottom left); page 6 (left); page 6 (bottom); page 7 (right);
   pages 8–9 (bottom); page 10 (bottom); pages 12–13 (bottom);
   pages 14–15; pages 18–19 (main); page 20 (top); page 20 (center);
   page 22 (center); pages 26–27; pages 28–29 (main); page 28
   (center); page 29 (left); page 33; page 36; page 37 (left); page 46;
   page 47 (left); pages 48–49; page 51 (top); page 58; page 59
Superstock: page 1 (center); page 34
U.S. Environmental Protection Agency: page 53
U.S. Fish and Wildlife: page 39 (bottom); page 40; page 43;
   page 44; page 45
Wikipedia Creative Commons (public domain): page 20 (bottom);
   page 22 (top); page 22 (bottom); page 37 (right); page 50 (left);
   page 51 (bottom)

Library and Archives Canada Cataloguing in Publication

Down, Susan Brophy
   Legally green : careers in environmental law / Susan Brophy Down.

(Green-collar careers)
Includes index.
Issued also in electronic format.
ISBN 978-0-7787-4857-1 (bound).--ISBN 978-0-7787-4868-7 (pbk.)

   1. Environmental law--Vocational guidance--Juvenile literature.
2. Environmental protection--Vocational guidance--Juvenile literature.
3. Environmentalists--Vocational guidance--Juvenile literature. I. Title.
II. Series: Green-collar careers

K3585.D69 2011   j344.04'6   C2011-903269-4

Library of Congress Cataloging-in-Publication Data

Down, Susan Brophy.
   Legally green careers in environmental law / Susan Brophy Down.
      p. cm. -- (Green-collar careers)
   Includes index.
   ISBN 978-0-7787-4857-1 (reinforced library binding : alk. paper) --
   ISBN 978-0-7787-4868-7 (pbk. : alk. paper) -- ISBN 978-1-4271-9721-4
   (electronic pdf)
   1. Environmental law--Vocational guidance--Juvenile literature.
I. Title.
   KF299.E6D69 2011
   344.7304'6--dc23

                       2011017983

Crabtree Publishing Company
www.crabtreebooks.com   1-800-387-7650

Printed in China/082011/TM20110511

Published in Canada
Crabtree Publishing
616 Welland Ave.
St. Catharines, Ontario
L2M 5V6

Published in the United States
Crabtree Publishing
PMB 59051
350 Fifth Avenue, 59th Floor
New York, New York 10118

Published in the United Kingdom
Crabtree Publishing
Maritime House
Basin Road North, Hove
BN41 1WR

Published in Australia
Crabtree Publishing
3 Charles Street
Coburg North
VIC 305

CONTENTS

A NEED FOR RESOURCES, A NEED FOR LAWS

Lawyer

If you look closely at this photo of a junkyard, you'll see plenty of everyday items. What's missing are computers, telephones, TVs, and other electronic devices that need special handling. Thanks to environmental laws designed to protect the planet's resources for centuries to come, these devices are forbidden from being dumped in ordinary landfills and junkyards.

Humans are having a huge impact on the planet. We continually want more and more of everything, from potato chips to new computers. We also want places to put all of our garbage and other waste. It hasn't always been this way. Tens of thousands of years ago, the earliest humans hunted, fished, gathered fruits and berries, and consumed water to survive. They used rocks, trees, earth, and the skins of animals to fashion tools, build shelters, and make clothes to keep themselves warm.

Paralegal   Activist

A simple item such as a potato chip bag may take 10 to 20 years to break down in a landfill, but only if it is exposed to sunlight. If not, it could take hundreds of years. Some scientists aren't even sure that certain plastic containers, such as those shown here choking an aquatic ecosystem, will ever break down.

Politician   Writer

Plenty to Go Around?

In more recent human history, people continued to figure out more ways to use the world's resources to improve their lives. People survived by using what they could find in nature. They threw away little and consumed only what they needed. There were fewer people than today, and they had plenty of resources to go around. People were able to use the resources they needed without causing significant damage to the planet.

Judge   Teacher

NO DUMPING
VIOLATORS WILL BE PROSECUTED

DO NO
DUM
REFUSE

NO LITTERING

Environmental laws can be extremely complex. For example, the Clean Air Act is hundreds of thousands of words long. They can also be as simple as any of these signs regulating the disposal of trash in a park!

CAREER PROFILE

SETTING HIGH STANDARDS: DIRECTING AN ENVIRONMENTAL LAW CENTER

I am at the New Mexico Environmental Law Center, a non-profit organization that depends upon grants and donations. I am the lead fundraiser, the director of the office, and a practicing attorney. We provide legal services to communities threatened by environmental degradation from landfills, roads, mines, oil and gas drilling, or extraction of groundwater resources.

Following graduation from Haverford College in Pennsylvania, I spent a year in VISTA (Volunteers in Service to America) in San Benito, Texas, helping low-income neighborhoods demand cleanup of damage caused by hurricane Beulah. I then graduated from Cornell University Law School in New York. After working for legal aid programs and the Consumer Protection Division of the New Mexico Attorney General's Office, I started the New Mexico Environmental Law Center.

I chose this career to help protect the environment and provide legal assistance and a voice to disadvantaged individuals and communities.

One of the most memorable occasions in my work occurred when I was involved in closing a medical waste incinerator that was polluting the air in a low-income immigrant community in southern New Mexico. I like making a difference.

Douglas Meiklejohn
Executive Director
New Mexico
Environmental
Law Center
Santa Fe,
New Mexico

GROWING NUMBERS, GROWING RESPONSIBILITY

The world's population reached 1 billion in 1804, and it is currently around 6.9 billion. Humans are expected to number between 7.5 and 10.5 billion by 2050. Our numbers on Earth are growing. As our numbers grow, so does our responsibility to monitor and control our impact on the health of the planet.

Today, particularly in Europe and North America, more people are using more of Earth's resources than ever. Fortunately, we have also come to realize the need to regulate, or control, how we use those resources. One way is to pass and enforce laws that protect the environment. This area of law is known as environmental law. Environmental law is critical to preserving Earth's resources. It is also an area that offers a wide variety of jobs for people who care about both the law and the health of our planet.

Right: You don't have to be an environmental scientist to recognize this all-too-common source of carbon dioxide (CO_2) and other greenhouse gas emissions—the car. The more we rely on vehicles run by fossil fuel-driven internal combustion engines, the greater the risks to the quality of Earth's atmosphere.

Technology–Making Life Better...at a Price

Today, we have sophisticated technology that our ancestors never could have imagined. Thanks to cars, buses, trains, ships, and airplanes, we can go just about anywhere in the world in a matter of hours. Computer-based inventions and gadgets keep us connected with the global community. In most parts of the world, we can obtain clothes, food, shelter, and water without having to produce things from scratch.

SO WHAT ARE FOSSIL FUELS?

Fossil fuels come from deep beneath Earth's surface. They started to develop millions of years ago when tiny marine plants and animals died and sank to the bottoms of rivers, lakes, and oceans. There, buried by sediment, they eventually decomposed into carbon. Over vast periods of time, they became converted to oil, coal, or gas.

Above: The use of offshore oil drilling rigs to extract fossil fuel supplies has been a subject of some controversy and debate, particularly following the 2010 BP oil spill in the Gulf of Mexico. The BP disaster took the lives of 11 workers and caused enormous harm to the environment in the Gulf and along the Gulf Coast. The disaster was the result of an explosion of a rig resembling the one shown here. This rig is drilling for oil and natural gas off the coast of Southern California.

The Tutuka Power Station in South Africa is shown here with five of its six units operating. Tutuka is a coal-fired power plant that is a key component in South Africa's electrical power grid. It is also run by a company that has one of the highest rates of carbon dioxide (CO_2) emissions on the planet.

On top of the financial cost, this convenience has come with an even greater price—risks to the health of our planet. Fossil fuels (gas, oil, and coal) provide the energy that makes most modern technology possible. When these fuels are burned, they power our homes, businesses, factories, and most modes of transportation. They also help generate the electricity that runs our computers and other machines.

Burning fossil fuels also releases carbon dioxide (CO_2) and other gases known as greenhouse gases into the atmosphere. Greenhouse gases have always been present in Earth's atmosphere. They play an important role in warming our planet and making life possible. In recent years, however, levels of greenhouse gases have been increasing. These gases have trapped more of the Sun's heat inside Earth's atmosphere. Most scientists feel that this increase in greenhouse gases is the main cause of global warming.

Two sources of contamination that have come under increased regulation in recent years are shown here. Above: Containers holding toxic chemicals, like these cans and drums lying in water in a landfill, must now be disposed of in special ways to avoid contaminating surrounding areas. Right: Pesticides, such as those sprayed onto crops, may be beneficial to farmers and other growers, but they may also contain substances that are harmful to plant, animal, and human life. They must be carefully tested, evaluated, and regulated before they can be used.

Climate change, the main cause of global warming on our planet, is believed to be one of the causes of extreme weather patterns that may bring on floods, hurricanes, or droughts. Climate change can also increase the rate at which ice melts at Earth's north and south poles. The melting of polar ice can result in flooding that puts low-lying communities and ecosystems at risk. Another problem with fossil fuels is that we are burning them so fast that supplies are running low. Energy sources such as wind, water, and the Sun are sustainable, or renewable. Unlike those resources, fossil fuels are limited. Once we use up the supplies of fossil fuel from deep beneath Earth's surface, they are gone forever. Some scientists believe that we will use up these supplies within the next 100 years!

Our Polluted Planet

In addition to carbon dioxide, burning fossil fuels releases other elements into the air. These include sulfur and nitrogen. When combined with fog or haze, these and other pollutants can create smog. Smog affects the atmosphere and the health of humans and other creatures that breathe in polluted air. When combined with air, water vapor, and sunshine, these pollutants can create acids that fall as rain or snow. This form of pollution is called acid rain. Acid rain can harm historic buildings, statues, and metal objects. It also poses a danger to water, soil, and the health of humans and other living things.

Of course, burning fossil fuels isn't the only cause of harm to planet Earth. Humans all over the world tend to live in "disposable" societies.

THERE OUGHT TO BE A LAW!

Most of us can think of an instance where something precious to us in nature was destroyed or taken away. Maybe your favorite playground or a nearby marsh was bulldozed to make room for a new condominium project. Maybe a beach or local lake became polluted, and you had to stop swimming there so you wouldn't become sick. Maybe a wooded area near you was cut down. Now, you have noticed that fewer birds, squirrels, and chipmunks come to feed in your back yard. These are just a few examples of the types of things that might be protected by more effective environmental laws.

People simply throw things away when they are finished using them. Trash finds its way into landfills, sewers, and waterways. There, substances that are difficult to break down, or decompose, might contaminate soil and groundwater for years or even centuries to come. Our cars, cities, factories, and hobbies create all kinds of pollution. Pesticides and other chemicals used to help grow plants contaminate the soil. They also pollute nearby rivers and lakes. Harmful chemicals and other substances have had a devastating impact on the environment.

Today, we are more aware of the effects of substances like these on our planet and on the health and safety of living things.

Think about this the next time you line up a shot with a pool cue, sit on outdoor furniture, or take notes with a pencil and paper: The wood used in these and countless other items may come from imperiled tropical rain forests. The logging industry is the main cause for the deforestation of tropical rain forests like the one shown here on Borneo, an island shared by Indonesia and Malaysia. Roads cut by logging companies through the habitats of endangered animals such as the orangutan (shown here) have put thousands of species of plants, mammals, birds, and insects at risk. Many of these roads are built illegally, and it is up to international environmental agencies and other organizations to prevent such illegal actions and to penalize those who commit them.

We recognize the value of reusing and recycling items once we're done with them. We now have laws, regulations, and organizations that control how people dispose of certain items.

A World in Need of Environmental Laws

On our roads we have stop signs and other traffic signals. Those rules are in place to keep everyone safe. If a car speeds through a red light, it puts others in danger. Also, the driver might be caught by the police and have to pay a fine.

We share our environment just as we share our roads, and we need laws to keep it safe, too.

"The fact is, if we are going to deal with the environmental crisis, someone needs to speak truth to power. Someone needs to speak for nature. And that's where you law students come in. Now, more than ever, nature needs advocates. Lawyers are ideally suited to this task of giving voice to the voiceless."

Calvin Sandborn,
Legal Director,
University of Victoria
Environmental Law Centre,
Victoria, British Columbia

Today, most people practice reusing and recycling things that they no longer need. Without laws and the regulations and agencies that enforce those laws, many people would probably not recycle. They might stop caring completely. What would the world be like without laws to control pollution? People would be able to dump garbage wherever they liked or throw everything away in landfills. Factories could pour toxic chemicals into rivers and lakes.

Logging companies could cut down forests without regard for the impact on nearby people and wildlife. Gasoline stations would not be required to keep their property free of dangerous chemicals and other toxins. Hunters could shoot animals in protected areas such as parks. Today, businesses must meet safety standards established by laws. These standards require businesses that use dangerous chemicals to clean up or replace contaminated soil and groundwater.

A Career for You?

As we prepare to examine the major areas of environmental law in this book, let's take a quick look at a few career options.

Researcher. Do you love to find answers and learn about new things? Do you find yourself spending hours researching and learning on the Internet or in the library? Do you have a knack for detail and a flair for detective work? Do you love to learn new things? If so, you'd probably make a good researcher. There are all kinds of job opportunities for researchers in legal firms, law libraries, government agencies, private companies, and environmental non-governmental organizations (eNGOs) such as Greenpeace or the World Wildlife Fund (WWF).

Politician. Governments are responsible for deciding whether a proposed law should become a new law. From town or city council member or mayor, to elected legislator, to the head of a state, provincial,

The choices are many and varied: performing research for a private firm or government agency; adding your voice as an environmental organizer or activist; working in a law office as a legal secretary, legal aid, or paralegal; teaching others; bringing environmental issues to light as a journalist or media professional; or serving the public as a lawmaker, prosecutor, or judge.

or even federal government, politicians have a lot of influence when it comes to changing the world. Maybe you already have some experience in this area. Did you ever run for class president or serve as an officer of your 4H club? Do you love public speaking and find it easy to convince others to follow causes that you believe in? If so, it sounds as if you might be a natural leader. The future depends on strong leaders with a passion for everything green. Go for it!

Paralegal, Legal Secretary, or Administrative Assistant. Paralegals help lawyers prepare cases by assisting with research and preparing legal documents. Legal secretaries and administrative assistants are masters of organization. They help prepare legal documents and manage communication materials, and they usually have a knack for learning software applications. If this sounds like something you'd enjoy, you'll find yourself with plenty of job opportunities!

Judge. Do you have a strong sense of justice? Has anyone ever told you that you are calm, fair, and good at seeing both sides to every story? Judges have the final say in court cases. They must listen to all parties involved in a case and decide who is right and who is wrong. There are all kinds of legal environmental issues in the world today, so there is a huge demand for judges who started their careers in environmental law.

Writing, Communications, and Media. Lawyers don't spend all their time in courtrooms. They publish articles about environmental issues for magazines and newspapers. They write and edit professional papers for legal publications. They even write books. Some specialize in environmental journalism, using their law degrees to special advantage. Others turn to communications. They may be hired by governments and corporations to handle media relations. Some are good at using their communications or technical skills on the Internet. Some even pick up a camera and become documentary filmmakers and photographers!

WORKING FOR ENVIRONMENTAL JUSTICE

Environmental justice is a relatively new field related to law. The U.S. Environmental Protection Agency defines environmental justice as "the fair treatment and meaningful involvement of all people regardless of race, color, national origin, or income with respect to the development, implementation, and enforcement of environmental laws, regulations, and policies." This means that people in the environmental justice field work for all people to have access to a safe, clean, and healthy environment. It also means that all people, regardless of their status or background, should have an equal voice in deciding on policies that affect their environment.

Even if you don't go on to become a lawyer, there are plenty of opportunities for people with talents in writing and other forms of communication when it comes to the environment and the law. After all, the pen (or these days, sometimes the camera) is mightier than the sword!

Activist. You are not afraid to fight for what you believe in, and you believe in a clean, safe world where everyone has access to healthy food, fresh water, and clean air. You are also good at rallying others to help your cause. With a background in law, you can become a powerful voice for change. By the way, lawyers can be activists, too.

In this photo, members of the environmental activist group Greenpeace form a blockade cutting off access to one of paper manufacturer Kimberly-Clark's factories in Ontario. This action took place during a period that culminated in a historic agreement in 2009 between Kimberly-Clark and Greenpeace. According to the agreement, the manufacturer of Kleenex-brand paper products pledged not to purchase wood pulp from certain environmentally sensitive forests in Ontario unless strict ecological standards were met. With its lobbying, publicity, email, and other campaigns, Greenpeace has long been one of the world's best-known environmental non-governmental organizations (eNGOs).

Teacher/Professor. Can't decide between teaching and law? You can do both! With a background in environmental law, you can teach high school, become a university or college professor, or educate government or corporate employees about environmental laws.

A Chance to Set Things Right

As problems here on Earth expand, so do the opportunities to set things right. Are you considering a career in environmental law? If so, you will be helping to create, defend, and enforce laws that protect the water, land, air, and all the living things that call Earth home. You will become an advocate for the safety and health of humans and nature alike!

ENGOS TO THE RESCUE

Just as guard dogs protect houses and people, some groups are watchdogs for the environment. They are not part of the government, and they aren't companies. They are special independent groups known as eNGOs, which is short for a bigger mouthful: environmental non-governmental organizations. These groups are made up of concerned citizens, including many volunteers. Often they are the first ones to bring attention to a pollution problem or wildlife concern in the community. They rely on donations from people who believe in their important work.

CHAPTER 2

MAKING LAWS

This adult whooping crane is one of a pair that is being used to breed chicks to help boost the population of whooping cranes worldwide. It is shown here feeding in a pond at the International Crane Foundation in Baraboo, Wisconsin.

Wearing a T-shirt that says "Save the Whales" may make you look great, and it gets a message across, but it won't do much to actually help the animals. To protect the environment, we need to do more than make a fashion statement! We need strict laws that everyone follows. Creating laws can be complicated and can sometimes take years. The results, however—a cleaner world—are worth all the effort.

Getting On Board with Environmental Laws

Most countries have two main kinds of environmental laws. Pollution control laws keep the water, land, and air from becoming contaminated with chemicals that can harm us. Resource management laws protect natural ecosystems, such as forests or lakes. These are the laws, for example, that keep people from cutting down trees in parks that have been set aside for camping. They also protect certain animals against hunters and smugglers. If an animal is rare, or endangered, allowing it to be hunted without protection could cause its numbers to become dangerously low. It might even mean it could become extinct, or disappear completely.

Where Do Laws Come from?

Like all laws, environmental laws get their start in a variety of ways. They can begin as good ideas, and they can start at any level. Let's say, for example, that people are dumping old computers and tires in the trash when they should be recycled. By passing a law, elected city officials can change the public's behavior.

SPECIAL STATUS FOR ANIMALS

The growth of human populations may cause some bird and animal populations to grow smaller and smaller. The American bison (buffalo) once galloped across the North American plains in huge herds. Hunting by European settlers reduced their numbers. Most of the surviving bison are living on ranches, parks, and wildlife preserves. The passenger pigeon wasn't even that lucky. Even though there were billions flying around 300 years ago, hunters killed every one. The last one died in a zoo in 1914.

Countries often have to work together to save these animals. Only 21 whooping cranes were left in the whole world in the 1940s. Whooping cranes breed in northern Canada and spend the summer in Texas, so the Canadian and U.S. governments worked together to protect the cranes. Thanks to the efforts of both governments, about 500 beautiful whooping cranes are alive today.

Special laws, like the Species at Risk Act in Canada and the Endangered Species Act in the United States, identify animal and plant species that are at risk. To help protect these species, these acts have provided the following labels that identify wildlife whose numbers are at risk:

- **Threatened:** species whose population will grow smaller in the future.

- **Endangered:** species that are very rare and that will become extinct if not protected.

- **Extinct:** species that have no living members left on the planet.

TIRED OF TIRES

There are plenty of reasons to be concerned about the effect of stockpiles of tires on human health and the environment. Because of their shape, tires can collect rainwater, attracting mosquitoes and rats. Tires also have the strength and ability to retain heat. This makes them prone to igniting, creating blazes that may take months to put out.

According to the U.S. Environmental Protection Agency (EPA), burning tires can break down into numerous harmful chemical components. These chemicals endanger both the ground and the air. One particularly troublesome component of tires is oil, and one tire can produce up to two gallons (7.5 liters) of oil! That oil, in turn, is itself inflammable. It can also seep into the ground, polluting underlying soil and groundwater.

Today, thanks mostly to state and local scrap management programs and regulations, the estimated number of stockpiled tires in the United States has gone down from 700–800 million in 1984 to an estimated 275 million.

Once the need for a law is established, the law itself is developed from extensive research. There are many, many questions for researchers to answer before an environmental law can be passed. For example, lawmakers need to know which chemicals are bad for our air and waterways. That list might come from scientists who study the effects of gases and chemicals on air and water. It might also come from biologists who track animal and fish populations. The results of these studies can be the basis for fair laws.

It takes months and sometimes years to get citizens and business people together to agree on what environmental restrictions are necessary. Once a law is passed, it may

In addition to ruining the beauty of a landscape, stockpiles of tires are safety risks and pose threats to health and the environment.

be modified, or changed, to meet changing circumstances. The Clean Air Act is an important U.S. law that was passed in the 1970s to protect the air from harmful pollutants. It has been changed several times since then, and now the "simple" version is 293 pages long!

Laying Down the Law

Laws go through different stages, and they often have different names as they are created and modified. Sometimes they start as policies, or ways of thinking or acting, and end up with a lot of regulations, or rules. Here are a few terms to know as you read about environmental law:

• A *policy* is a general way of thinking or a course of action. *Education is important for all children:* That might be a simple policy. A government may create policies after talking to stakeholders, or the people and companies affected by the government's decisions.

THE GREAT SMOG DISASTER

The smog disaster in London in December 1952 was caused by coal burning and other industrial gases that mixed with a heavy fog. The smog was so thick that it was impossible to see very far ahead, and road traffic, trains, and airplanes had to stop running. In fact, the air was so foul that many people had breathing problems, and more than 4,000 people died. In the aftermath of this event, the British government passed the Clean Air Act in 1956.

A visitor in London wears a smog mask only months after thousands lost their lives during the deadly 1952 smog disaster. Officials had advised residents and visitors to use caution in venturing outside during this period of thick fog in the event of another smog alert.

In 1970, the U.S. government passed the National Environmental Policy Act. This was the government's way of saying that we have to consider the environment for certain types of projects, such as building roads or running a nuclear plant. According to this act, every federal agency would be required to write an environmental impact statement explaining what new projects would do to the environment.

• A *bill* is a preliminary, or draft, version of a law that is presented to federal and state (or, in Canada, provincial) governments for approval. Lawmakers may argue over the bill and then vote on it. If the majority agrees, then it will become an act.

• An *act* is a law (also called a *statute)* that has been voted on and approved by the government. An act is a general law

that will often identify a certain group to enforce the rules and create regulations.

- *Regulations* are the specific rules that tell you exactly what you can and cannot do. Let's say the government wants to protect a lake from too much fishing. The government may create regulations to achieve that goal. These regulations may state that each person needs a fishing license and can only catch one or two fish every week. The U.S. Environmental Protection Agency (EPA) is the main group that writes many regulations such as these.

- A *bylaw* (also known as an ordinance) is passed by local governments in towns and cities. Bylaws are often based on federal or state acts.

- An *amendment* is a change to an existing act. The Clean Air Act has been amended twice since it was passed in 1970. An act is sometimes changed because the law needs to be stricter to catch more offenders.

CAREER PROFILE

TEACHING LAWMAKING SKILLS AS AN ATTORNEY

My job combines two of my passions: the environment and international travel. I studied physics, anthropology, and math at Michigan State University. I then earned my master's degree in Physics at the University of Texas. Scientific research wasn't the type of job I wanted, however, so I got a law degree at the Northwestern School of Law of Lewis and Clark Law College.

As part of my job at the Environmental Law Institute (ELI) in Washington, D.C., I do a lot of talking—to my colleagues about new ideas, to funders about donations, and to researchers about our projects. Once a month I travel to conferences or training courses or to do research or help countries draft their laws.

I am most proud when I am able to change how people look at an issue. ELI has helped South Sudan draft laws on people's right to a healthy environment. We also helped Liberia create a framework for environmental law.

Figure out your objective and create a map to that objective. Be persistent. People succeed because they work very hard, and they're not going to be working hard for something they don't like.

Carl Bruch
Senior Attorney and Co-director of
International Programs
Environmental Law Institute
Washington, D.C.

From developing new highways and bridges to constructing a waterslide within the natural landscape of an amusement park such as Lake Compounce in Bristol, Connecticut (shown here), building projects must measure up to a series of rules and regulations designed to protect the environment and natural ecosystems.

Where bills become laws (top to bottom): the U.S. Congress in Washington, D.C.; the British Parliament in London, England; and the Canadian Parliament in Ottawa, Ontario.

How Do Laws Become Laws?

Most important environmental laws start at the federal level, but they can also be passed at the state or provincial level.

In the United States, a bill is introduced by members of the U.S. Congress. Congress is the legislative, or lawmaking, branch of the government. After a lot of discussion, the bill is voted on by both houses of Congress—the House of Representatives and the Senate. If a majority (more than 50 percent) of the lawmakers in each house votes in favor, the bill is passed on to the president to sign. The president can approve the bill or veto it (disapprove it). If the president approves the bill, it becomes a law. Examples of major environmental laws in the United States include the Clean Air Act, the Clean Water Act, and the National Environmental Policy Act.

In the United Kingdom, or UK, the legislative part of the government is called Parliament. It is made up of the House of Commons and the House of Lords. A bill can be introduced in either of the houses. To pass into law, the bill goes through three readings. During this process, the lawmakers can debate and make changes to the bill. After that, the lawmakers vote. If a majority approves the bill, it receives royal assent. This means that the bill is signed into law by the queen.

The Environmental Protection Act is one example of an important law that protects the environment in the UK.

Canada makes laws in a way that is similar to that of the UK. The bill goes through three readings, and then members can vote to pass it into law. The Parliament of Canada is made up of two bodies—the House of Commons and the Senate. Royal assent is given by the governor general on behalf of the queen. Some important laws in Canada include the Canadian Environmental Protection Act and the Fisheries Act.

Regulations

In addition to writing the rules, lawmakers must decide on the penalties for breaking the law. In the case of major damage, such as an oil spill, the penalty can be a very large fine, sometimes millions of dollars. Companies could be forced to pay for the cleanup as well. People can also go to jail for harming the environment.

Slow and Steady

Deciding on our environmental laws can take years. Clean air laws have existed in the United States since 1955. The objectives of the first laws, however, were mostly to provide rules for performing research on the environment. It wasn't until 1970 that the government passed the Clean Air Act with tougher rules on pollution.

DISASTER CREATES CHANGE

A river catching fire? It sounds crazy, but it happened—several times—in Cleveland, Ohio. The Cuyahoga River was so full of oil, chemicals, and trash floating on it that the whole mess actually caught fire! The biggest fire was in 1952. The most publicized fire, however, was in 1969. This is the one that led to the movement to create water-pollution-control commissions, agreements, and laws in both the United States and Canada, particularly around the Great Lakes.

It sometimes takes a full-blown catastrophe to get lawmakers to change laws. In that same year, 1969, an oil spill from a drilling platform off the California coast created a huge oil slick off Santa Barbara. People were so horrified that soon after, the government created new environmental laws.

Firefighters on a bridge over the Cuyahoga River in Cleveland spray water on a tugboat that has been caught in a blaze that started in an oil slick on the river. The November 1952 fire swept over the docks of the Great Lakes Towing Company, destroying three tugs, three buildings, and the ship repair yards.

THE RETURN OF CLEAR WATER

What can the members of a community do if their drinking water becomes contaminated? Health inspectors in Santa Monica, California, discovered a dangerous chemical in the city's water wells in 1996. They determined that the chemical, a gasoline additive, was leaking from underground storage tanks at local gas stations. As a result, officials made the oil companies pay to clean up the contamination and buy drinking water from northern California and the Colorado River while the city improved its water treatment plant to purify the well water. Following the events in Santa Monica, California banned the additive from gasoline sold in the state. After that, many other states decided to do the same thing. Finally, in 2010, Santa Monica citizens started using water from their local wells again. By 2020, officials plan to be water self-sufficient by providing 100 percent of the water for the community. That's a green success story!

Global Problems Require Global Solutions

Problems such as climate change and air, ground, and water pollution don't stop at a nation's border. The huge environmental issues facing our planet affect all of us, and they cannot be fixed by any one country alone.

Each country has to learn to cooperate if we are going to create a healthier world. The Canadian government has signed more than 130 treaties on everything from hazardous waste to endangered species and climate change. These treaties are bilateral (between two countries) or multilateral (between several countries).

This is why international environmental organizations and programs exist—to help nations work together and cooperate with one another. One of these programs is the United Nations Environment Programme (UNEP). UNEP coordinates other UN environmental programs and activities. It also helps countries create laws and programs of their own to protect the environment. One way it does this is by making nations aware of laws around the planet. It also suggests ways that nations can agree on protecting Earth.

By choosing a career in environmental law, you can help bring about new laws that improve the environment in your city, in your country, or even around the world!

Indonesian activists from the Center for Orangutan Protection (COP) protest against plans to convert forests to a palm oil plantation in Jakarta, Indonesia, in February 2010. At the time of the protests, Indonesia was hosting a gathering of the United Nations Environment Programme (UNEP). The goal of the conference was to help create a political declaration on significant environmental issues. The activists, dressed as characters from the movie *Avatar*, were urging the government to stop illegal forest clearance and save orangutans.

Librarians must have an appreciation for research and an understanding of available knowledge in both the world of publishing and electronic data sources. Those qualities, plus a willingness to help people get through the tremendous amount of information they face in most libraries, are essential ingredients to becoming a librarian.

CAREER PROFILE

LAYING THE FOUNDATION: LAW LIBRARIAN

I am very aware of environmental issues. My husband and I use solar power to run the house we built, and we grow our own food. I was hired as a reference librarian at Vermont Law School. Now I am the environmental law librarian, and I have been inspired by students and faculty to make a difference.

Lawyers can't do anything without first having information. Librarians can help because they are experts at accessing information. I have a bachelor's degree in Psychology from the University of Connecticut. I also have two master's degrees, one in Library Science and one in Liberal Studies.

I teach a course in advanced environmental legal research. I also go into classes and teach research techniques. When faculty members and students ask for help, I work with them to find what they need. In the library, I am the one who selects the new books and electronic resources for our collection. I am creating an environmental database of free Web sources. I love my job because there are always new challenges.

Christine Ryan
Law Librarian and
Adjunct Professor
Vermont Law School
South Royalton, Vermont

EDUCATION AND CAREERS

For most jobs in environmental law, you must have special training at a college or university. Careers in environmental law may include, of course, becoming a lawyer. Other areas related to environmental law can give you a chance to help the environment and offer a lot of adventure as well. These include teaching, journalism, and working at various jobs in a law firm other than actually becoming a practicing lawyer.

From photography to freelance writing, interviewing, and filmmaking—as well as radio, TV, and newspaper reporting— there are many paths leading to careers in environmental journalism.

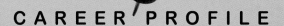

INDEPENDENT ENVIRONMENTAL JOURNALIST

I earned a bachelor's degree in Molecular Biology at McGill University. After that, I earned a master's degree in Science, Health, and Environmental Journalism at New York University. When I graduated, I worked as a magazine writer. Gradually, I started to get tired of writing about problems. I wanted to write about solutions.

Since I work for myself, I can do a lot of different projects. I might have three or four stories on the go at once. I write freelance articles for publications such as the *Sunday Times* of London, and I have been a radio commentator. I have taught environmental journalism at university, and I have written two books.

The most exciting stories are pieces for which I've traveled abroad. I have gone to Libya to write about power systems and to France to write about managing nuclear waste systems. One of the most exciting and fun stories I did was a piece on electric bicycles in China.

To be a journalist you need curiosity, determination, and a belief in the role of the press and the right to information.

Peter Fairley
Freelance Writer
Victoria, British Columbia

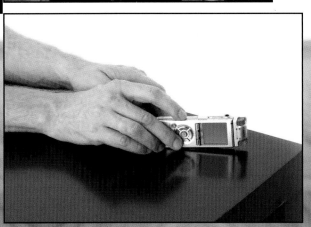

Environmental journalist Peter Fairley visits the site of a subject he is writing about—an electric bicycle factory in Shanghai, China.

Many Paths into Law

There are many different and exciting choices for careers in environmental law. As a teacher, you might offer courses that are related to the environment and the law. As a journalist, you might find yourself doing research and reporting on the effects of laws on the environment. Part of your job might be to do investigative reporting on whether corporations are complying with environmental rules and regulations. A background in journalism or English might help give you the credentials to work for a newspaper or a publisher. As a freelance writer or journalist, you would be able to have more flexibility and creative control over your choice of subjects than if you worked in an office.

You don't have to be a lawyer to teach, advocate for, or write about environmental law, but it doesn't hurt! Many people who work on behalf of people and environmental issues become lawyers and then use their legal background in other jobs.

Lawyer Tim Cooke-Hurle reviews a medical scan with the victim of an illegal toxic dump in Ivory Coast, Africa. Victims and their attorneys claimed that a large multinational oil-trading company, Trafigura, illegally dumped hundreds of tons of contaminated oil waste in landfills around Abidjan, the largest city in Ivory Coast, in 2006. Exposure to the toxic waste killed 16 people and caused 95,000 people to seek medical care. Prior to trial, the company agreed to a financial settlement with about 30,000 people who had been harmed in one of the worst pollution disasters in recent history.

French lawyers wait to hear the verdict in the trial of the sinking of the oil tanker *Erika* off the coast of France in 1999. When the ship broke up during a storm, it split in two, sank, and released thousands of tons of oil into the sea. Killing marine life and polluting the shores around Brittany, France, the spill was one of the greatest environmental disasters ever to hit the nation. In 2008, Total S.A., the multinational oil company that operated the *Erika*, was ordered to compensate all the victims of the spill as well as pay for the cleanup operation. In 2010, the company lost its appeal of the decision.

Becoming a Legal Eagle

Choosing to study law can lead to opportunities to work in countries all over the world. Most environmental lawyers practice what is called public interest law. This means they work for the good of the community against pollution. If you are a quick thinker and you like to convince people to be on your side, law could be the career for you.

Lawyers can choose to work for themselves or with other lawyers in a large company. In TV dramas, lawyers are always in the courtroom. If you like to perform, that could be your choice. Many lawyers prefer to work behind the scenes for a government department or agency, however. There, they can help shape public policy by writing the laws and regulations.

CAREER PROFILE

LEARNING LEGAL: BECOMING AN ENVIRONMENTAL LAWYER

This is my first year as a law student. I study various aspects of the law so I will have a broad understanding. In the future I will get to have more hands-on experiences with practicing the law.

On a typical day, I wake up and read my assignments. In class, the professor calls on students to talk about what they think the reading means. You never know when you're going to be called on, so you always have to be prepared.

Environmental law is a hot topic, and there will be more need for people to understand and apply regulations as well as help shape them. Resources, even in North America, are becoming more limited, so it will be important to have people who can keep an eye on them and protect them.

Before I entered law school, I was an editor. My college degree is in English and Secondary Education, and I have a master's in Writing and Publishing. If you have strong reading and writing skills and like to solve problems, this would be a good area for you. You have to enjoy research and thinking about complex issues, too.

Tea Benduhn
Law Student
Marquette University
School of Law
Milwaukee, Wisconsin

INVESTIGATIVE JOURNALISM: DIGITAL DUMPING

Ten journalism students and their professor at the University of British Columbia won an Emmy Award in 2010 for a news documentary called *Ghana: Digital Dumping Ground.* They traveled to Africa to find out what happens to the computers and cell phones that people throw away. After a lot of investigative research, including secretly filming the people who buy and sell used computers, they put the story together. The film showed the environmental impact of our digital garbage. It was shown on PBS. The ten students have graduated and are now working as journalists.

Studying after High School

Depending on your goals after high school, you can choose a college or university for some environmental training. Most two-year colleges have courses for paralegals and programs in communications or public relations. If you want to go into journalism, you can study that right away or take journalism classes in conjunction with other courses at either a two-year or four-year school. Taking English is never a bad idea if you plan to go into writing or editing.

If you have your heart set on law school, you will need a bachelor's degree first, which normally takes four years. While you can study any subject you like, it's a good idea to take a few courses in subjects such as political science (how government works), history, or economics. It is also very helpful to take courses in sciences if it is the environment you are interested in.

This disquieting scene of digital dumping in Ghana was the focus of an award-winning documentary by a group of journalism students in 2010. Workers from poverty-stricken regions of Ghana collect parts of electronic devices from Europe and North America. These parts are burned to recover copper and other metals, which are then sold to buyers who send the copper to China or India.

Besides being a lawyer, there are jobs in law offices for other members of a legal team. Paralegals, law clerks, and legal secretaries all help lawyers prepare a complicated case. A paralegal has taken college courses in litigation (courtroom proceedings), corporate law, and real estate. In most U.S. states and Canadian provinces, paralegals assist the lawyers. In some places, such as Ontario, they can work independently, with more individual responsibility.

The Route to Law School

There are two basic steps in order to get into law school and earn a law degree. In the United States and Canada, students first must earn their four-year bachelor's degree. They then must take the Law School Admission Test (LSAT). The scores on this exam will be sent with the application to law school. Good scores usually mean that more schools will accept the candidate. This test can be taken more than once, and universities offer special courses to help students prepare for the LSAT.

Law school usually takes three years of study. During that time, students learn about the laws in their state or province as well as federal laws.

Performing research for a law degree means studying historic law cases, most of which are available online.

Students also learn how to do research and prepare a case to take to court. If students choose environmental law, they might take courses on land use or international law and climate change rules.

There are many facets in a lawyer's typical day. The one that is probably best known is arguing a case in front of a judge or jury. Another, equally important one is preparing for cases at one's desk. This can happen in a private law firm, in the legal department for a large corporation, or in a prosecutor's or public defender's office.

A Lawyer by Any Other Name

Law degrees have different names depending on what country and what university they are from. In the United States, the degree is called the Juris Doctor (J.D.). In Canada, most schools offer a bachelor's degree in Law (LL.B.), but some schools offer J.D. degrees. The University of Detroit (in Michigan) and the University of Windsor (in Ontario), which are on opposite sides of the U.S-Canadian border near the Detroit River, offer a joint J.D. degree for people who want to practice in both countries.

Lawyers can also earn a master's degree in Law (LL.M.). This is for people who already have a law degree and want more specialized courses. Law degrees can be mixed and matched with other programs. For example, Vermont Law School offers a combined J.D. degree with a master's degree in Environmental Law and Policy.

Even lawyers have a lot of different names for themselves. These usually depend on the country they practice in. In the UK and Canada, a lawyer may be known as a barrister or a solicitor. A barrister is a lawyer who goes to court and appears before a judge for a client, and a solicitor is a lawyer who handles other legal matters. In Canada, lawyers qualify to do both jobs at once. In the UK, there are separate licensing rules for each job. In the United States, a lawyer is also known as an attorney.

GET CERTIFIED AS AN ENVIRONMENTAL PROFESSIONAL

A web of environmental regulations now exists, and that means trained assessors are needed to report on all the rules. Many projects require environmental impact assessments before they can go ahead. These projects might include building new roads or redeveloping old industrial sites to build new homes.

People with training in environmental sciences, engineering, or other related fields can be certified as environmental professionals by the Environmental Careers Organization of Canada (ECO). In the United States, there are several options, depending on the area. For example, California has a list of registered environmental assessors who work with companies to make sure they comply with the laws.

Reaching the Bar

After graduation, there are more hurdles to jump over before you can call yourself a lawyer. Graduates must take a bar exam in the state or province where they plan to practice. After passing the bar exam in the United States, you become an attorney-at-law. However, Canadian law graduates have to "article," or serve a period of training, with a legal firm for about a year before they can take the bar exams to become licensed lawyers. In the UK, graduates must also complete a period of training.

Go For It

Environmental law is becoming such a big field that many universities offer students a chance to specialize. There are some fine schools that have special programs. Many environmental law schools have offices where you can help on real cases. Start thinking about it now, choose the right classes and study hard when the time comes, and you'll be on the path to a career in environmental law before you know it!

A day in the life of a lawyer can mean meeting with clients or witnesses, being out in public at a courthouse, working behind the scenes in a law office, and more. Environmental law, where rules and regulations are growing so quickly, requires dedication to hard work and putting in long hours.

WHAT IS THE BAR?

Centuries ago in the UK, a wooden bar was set up in a courtroom to separate the audience from the judges and officials. Only qualified people could enter this part of the room to argue their cases. "The bar" is still part of legal language today. In the United States, lawyers call becoming a licensed attorney being "admitted to the bar." In Canada, it is referred to as being "called to the bar."

Traditionally, the "bar" meant a bar, gate, or partition separating the area reserved for judges, lawyers, and other court officials from the public seating area. Today, "the bar" refers to licensed lawyers as a group or to the practice of law as a profession.

CHAPTER 4

INVESTIGATION AND ENFORCEMENT

Skimmer boats gather oil and begin a controlled burn on the surface of the Gulf of Mexico in an effort to control a massive spill following the explosion of the *Deepwater Horizon* oil rig on April 20, 2010. The explosion on the rig claimed 11 workers' lives and created an uncapped well at the ocean floor. Three months and hundreds of thousands of gallons of spilled oil later, the gusher was finally brought under control. The investigation into the explosion and subsequent environmental disaster went on for months, however. The investigation culminated in a lawsuit by the U.S. government against the energy giant BP and other companies involved in the spill. The objective of the suit was to collect payment involved in the cleanup and environmental recovery.

If you choose a career as an environmental Sherlock Holmes, you'll quickly discover that there are many different ways to solve a case. Investigators are trained to collect evidence on the toxin dumpers, the forest choppers, and the hunters and poachers who illegally capture, smuggle, or kill threatened or endangered species. Investigators and assessors also report on the effects of natural disasters such as hurricanes, floods, or earthquakes as well as human-made disasters such as oil spills and nuclear accidents.

The Profit Motive

There are huge profits to be made on illegal activities that can harm an ecosystem. Some people are willing to pay a lot of cash for skins from a tiger or ivory from an elephant. Other people are willing to pay to dump toxic waste or cut trees illegally. Many of these environmental crimes are committed by organized crime networks. That means they usually commit other crimes, such as document fraud, bribery, and corruption as well as gun and people smuggling. Criminals are very secretive, so even though the results are obvious, it is sometimes difficult to figure out who is responsible. That's why we need well-trained investigators who can solve the cases and bring those responsible to justice.

Typical of the wildlife affected by the BP spill is this pelican found covered with oil on Grande Isle, Louisiana. It is being cleaned by a team devoted to rescuing and rehabilitating wild birds, especially those affected by oil spills.

Inspectors examine a vast assortment of wildlife products at JFK International Airport in New York. These items are likely to be traded illegally by poachers, smugglers, and traffickers. These items include products made out of tusks, horns, skins, and even the bodies of animals that are protected by international laws.

IFAW—SAVING WILD ANIMALS

Local wildlife officers in the Caribbean recently caught smugglers who had over 1,000 parrots and monkeys brought illegally from the South American nation of Venezuela. These enforcement officers were trained by the International Fund for Animal Welfare (IFAW). The group's mission to investigate and expose harmful wildlife practices around the world includes campaigns to stop the illegal hunting of tigers and elephants.

To fight serious criminals, environmental enforcement officers need some of the same skills as police officers or other types of investigators. They learn how to collect evidence, work with hazardous materials, interrogate (interview) suspects, and how to testify (tell their stories) in court. An elite group of Environmental Protection Agency (EPA) investigators are called special agents. Like police officers, they can carry firearms and make arrests.

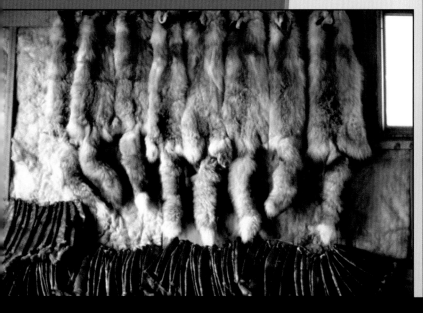

Above: A group of fox skins were confiscated for having been trafficked in violation of international trade laws.

Right: A U.S. Fish and Wildlife law enforcement officer displays illegal wildlife trade items seized at U.S. ports.

Watching with an Eagle Eye

Officials must first identify the problem, whether it is disappearing birds or illegal logging or polluting. This is called gathering intelligence. The person who might see the first evidence of a crime could be a U.S. Fish and Wildlife Service officer, a park warden, or a coast guard employee. The information might come from a tip from a local resident or another citizen who has seen something suspicious.

INTERNATIONAL CRIME FIGHTING—INTERPOL

When an environmental crime involves people smuggling animals from one country to another or a ship illegally spilling waste oil into the ocean, catching the people responsible requires international cooperation. That's where INTERPOL comes in. INTERPOL (The International Criminal Police Organization) is the world's largest international police group. Started in 1923, it now has 188 countries as members. In addition to fighting drug trafficking, terrorism, and other types of crime, INTERPOL offers environmental training.

The group has practical resources such as a database of information on known criminals as well as DNA and fingerprint samples. INTERPOL also has guidebooks on how to interrogate smugglers and how to look for hidden smuggled goods.

An INTERPOL regional bureau chief (left) and Kenya Wildlife Service (KWS) ranger look at tusks from elephants illegally killed for their ivory. With the help of the KWS and other Kenyan law enforcement groups, the 2009 INTERPOL-coordinated operation against poachers resulted in the seizure of over 1,250 pounds (567 kilograms) of carved and raw ivory in Kenya alone.

THE ENVIRONMENTAL INVESTIGATION AGENCY

In the 1980s, wild birds were caught by the millions in African countries and then smuggled to North America to be sold as pets. Investigators from the EIA went undercover. They found that most of the birds died before they reached their destination. To eliminate the smuggling completely, they convinced more than 150 airlines to stop carrying birds. The EIA also worked with the U.S. government on the Wild Bird Conservation Act. Stopping bird smuggling is just one of their global success stories!

The Enforcers

Enforcement officers gather information, conduct inspections, and investigate any suspected cases of damage to the environment such as pollution or harm to wildlife. They might work with local officials or international police groups such as INTERPOL.

In Canada and the United States, authorities recommend that people interested in working for the federal environmental agencies study for a college diploma in environmental science or criminology. If you are hired by a group such as Environment Canada, you will take several more weeks of training.

Specialized courses are also available at the Federal Law Enforcement Training Center in the United States. International groups such as the United Nations and the Environmental Investigation Agency (EIA) provide guidebooks and training. The EIA publishes case studies on successful operations all over the world.

A U.S. Fish and Wildlife Service officer inspects an Asian box turtle that arrived in a shipment at Miami International Airport. Turtle species that are rare or endangered may require special documentation and proof of their origins to be allowed to be traded internationally.

Inspecting the Scene

In the pollution-control field, a regular inspection of a factory or other business is the first step in environmental regulation. Companies that use toxic materials or create hazardous waste have to regularly report on their activities. If the inspections show that they don't meet certain regulations, then the inspector might give them a fine or take away their permits.

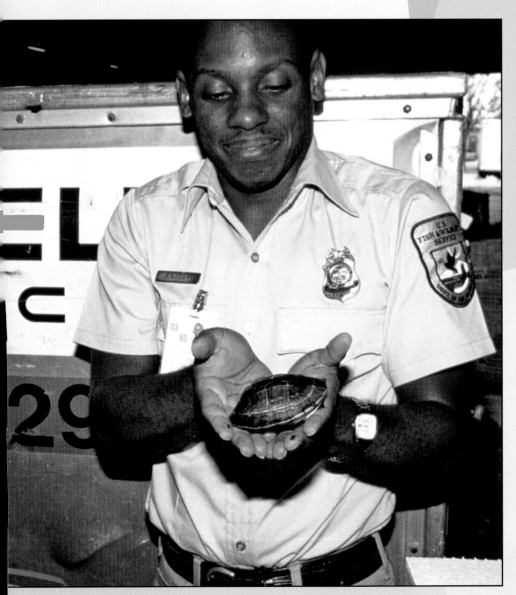

CAREER PROFILE

U.S. FISH AND WILDLIFE INSPECTOR

My job is to stop illegal wildlife trade and catch wildlife smugglers. I determine whether exotic animals or products made from them are allowed to enter or exit the United States. I check for permits and inspect the animals or products to identify them.

I took biology classes in high school and college. I also took law enforcement classes in college and volunteered to work with U.S. Fish and Wildlife Service Office of Law Enforcement. I planned to be a police officer, but then I became interested in conservation. Now I have the best of both worlds.

Inspectors do their work at air cargo warehouses, international airport passenger terminals, ocean ports, mail facilities, land border crossings, and other places. I look at shipments such as live lizards. I open the crate, and if they are a protected species that can't be imported, I'll seize them. Some may have gotten out of their containers, so I might have to catch them and put them back! Many years ago I was rammed by a lion during an inspection. I was not injured. He was a young lion and was being playful with me.

Tamesha Woulard
Wildlife Inspector
Office of Law Enforcement
U.S. Fish and Wildlife Service
Chicago, Illinois

UNDERCOVER WILDLIFE CRIME INVESTIGATOR: SPECIAL AGENT

I enforce U.S. wildlife conservation laws by investigating crimes against wildlife. I started my career with the service as a wildlife biologist. However, most special agents come from state game warden backgrounds or transfer from other federal law enforcement agencies to pursue a passion for wildlife conservation.

There is no average day. I may be working in the marsh looking for waterfowl poachers, digging through financial records to bring down an endangered species trafficker, reviewing evidence in a wolf-poisoning case, interviewing suspects, or testifying in court. We have a top-notch group of persistent investigators who find a way to catch the "bad guys" and protect our natural resources.

Each of our special agents combines two main fields of expertise: criminal investigation and natural resources management. We now have special agents who are computer forensics experts. The competition is stiff for jobs. All applicants must have a college degree, and most have advanced degrees or extensive job-related experience and a deep appreciation for natural resources.

**Special Agent
Office of Law Enforcement
U.S. Fish and Wildlife Service
(Note: Because Fish and Wildlife Service special agents often work undercover, this individual asked that his name and geographic location be withheld.)**

Investigating the Crime

Investigations are not the same as inspections. The purpose of an investigation is to collect evidence on suspected wrongdoing. An investigator, often with a police officer, can make a surprise visit to the business. They carry a search warrant, which is a permit issued by the court to enter the area and look for information. They might interview employees, copy documents, and take test samples for analysis. Sometimes they can seize other materials that they believe to be important.

U.S. Fish and Wildlife Service biologists take blood samples from a wolf after tranquilizing it and fitting it with a radio collar in Yellowstone National Park. The U.S. Endangered Species Act (ESA) protects certain wolves and other endangered wildlife species from being hunted, harmed, or imperiled. The collar will aid wildlife officers in tracking injured or killed animals and apprehending those suspected of harming them.

Gathering evidence is necessary so the authorities can prove their cases against the lawbreakers in court. Sometimes these investigations can take much longer than one visit to a factory. Perhaps the investigators have to study the situation over time and take photographs and videos, often with hidden cameras. Sometimes, investigators have to go undercover, which means they don't admit their true identities. They might pretend to be buyers of an endangered animal so they can get proof that these crimes are going on.

Crime Scene—Under the Microscope

Specialists are needed to work on some cases where scientific knowledge can help solve the mystery. For example, smugglers may claim that the animal parts in the shipment are not taken from endangered species.

Confiscated products made out of animal pelts. It isn't always clear whether the law has been followed or broken when certain animal products show up in international shipments. In cases where shippers may have mixed illegally traded animal parts with legitimate items, the shipment may have to be evaluated by forensics experts.

FUEL SPILL CULPRIT NABBED

Good detective work solved an environmental mystery a few years ago in Florida. A response team from the Florida Department of Environment discovered dead fish and an oil spill in a wildlife preserve. They analyzed the spill and determined that it was diesel fuel, and they traced the fuel back through the sewer system. Luckily, someone had taken a photo of a man pouring the fuel down a storm sewer. After the police charged him under the Clean Water Act and took him to court, he was sentenced to 15 months in jail. His company was fined almost $20,000 and had to pay another $20,000 to clean up the mess.

The criminals might have forged documents to make it seem legal. It's up to the investigating team to decide whether that is true. The team needs a scientist or even a veterinarian to examine forensic evidence. Do you like to do puzzles or play computer games in which you have to follow clues and make quick decisions? Maybe you would be a good investigator!

Good News for the Planet

Investigators are a vital part of environmental law enforcement. Their work can have a huge effect on the public. Sometimes a careful investigation into environmental wrongdoing

Two examples of oil and gasoline pollution, one related to water, the other to soil. Top: These swans are covered with oil dumped into a lake or pond. Bottom: What looks like a river running through a green space is actually a stretch of soil contaminated by oil and other toxic petrochemical products.

will convince countries to pass new laws. When people learn about the investigations through the media, that kind of exposure can be a powerful deterrent. Potential criminals will think again before they harm the environment and risk getting arrested.

A proper investigation can take months while the team collects the evidence, especially in an international case. By providing the evidence, investigators can help lawyers build a strong case against the people who try to harm the environment. Then the lawyers can take the next step of enforcing the law and recommending penalties such as fines or jail terms.

In March 1989, the *Exxon Valdez* oil tanker ran aground off the coast of Alaska, spilling hundreds of thousands of gallons of crude oil and contaminating both the waters and the shoreline. In the aftermath of this, the second-largest oil spill in U.S. history, it was necessary to investigate the area in order to determine responsibility for the spill and the cleanup. Here, a diver beneath a portion of the spill is part of the effort to assess the extent of the damage.

Investigating illegal dumping or other kinds of pollution may involve collecting evidence in the form of water samples.

BRINGING JUSTICE

Go to jail. Go directly to jail. Do not pass Go. If only protecting the environment were as easy as playing a game of Monopoly! After governments pass laws against harming the environment, and the investigators find the evidence of wrongdoing, the next step is to put those laws into action. Making sure environmental justice is done requires a group of dedicated legal professionals.

Obeying the Law

"Guilty!" booms the judge on the TV drama, and the sheriff leads the prisoner off to jail. In fact, this is not always the way the law works. There are many different types of punishments that governments can use to make people comply with (obey) the laws. After an inspection or an investigation reveals

Statues of Lady Justice, typically shown as she is here, adorn many courthouses all over the world. Based on classical images from ancient Greece and Rome, this figure holds a double-edged sword representing reason and justice and a set of scales representing the balance between truth and fairness. The blindfold represents impartiality and objectivity. These qualities are all considered virtues in our judicial system.

damage to the environment, polluters can face a series of penalties that get more and more serious.

Warnings First

As a first step, enforcement officers will give a warning that the company has violated the law. If things don't then improve, they will issue a ticket or even stop the operation of the business completely until the situation is fixed. These fines and penalties are handled by bodies that function like law courts. These bodies may be called many things, such as administrative courts or tribunals. The U.S. Environmental Protection Agency has its own independent office of administrative judges who make decisions on cases between the EPA and those regulated by the EPA laws.

Civil versus Criminal Law

In extreme cases where fines don't stop the environmental damage, someone has to prosecute the offenders (take them to court) when they are caught. In a courtroom, both sides— the accused polluter and the plaintiff, or accuser—have lawyers to argue on their behalf. A lawyer who is well prepared and skilled at presenting

Three scenes from a modern courtroom are shown here: an empty witness chair and judge's bench; a lawyer arguing his case passionately before a jury; and a judge presiding over the proceedings from the bench.

MINAMATA DISEASE— JAPAN'S WORST CASE OF INDUSTRIAL POLLUTION

In the 1950s, the residents in the small Japanese fishing village of Minamata got sick from a mysterious illness. Chisso Corporation had a factory in the area that produced a chemical used for making plastics. To make this chemical they had to use mercury, which was dumped into the bay, where it contaminated the fish. When the local people ate the fish, the mercury poisoning caused seizures, muscle spasms, and even death. Babies were born with abnormalities. The sickness became known as Minamata disease.

In 1956, a local doctor reported that it was the mercury from the Chisso factory that was making people sick. Despite that report, local and national governments failed to act on what had become a terrible environmental and human disaster, and Chiso continued to dump the chemicals until 1968. It took another 20 years before Japan's Supreme Court found the company and its executives guilty—and it wasn't until 2010 that the Japanese government made an out-of-court settlement with more than 2,000 victims.

convincing, logical arguments can make a big difference in the outcome of a case.

This process can take a long time, and it can be very expensive. The case might start at the state or provincial level. After the judge decides the case, the loser can appeal by asking another court to hear the argument. Some cases may eventually reach the Supreme Court, where nine judges decide together.

There are two parts to the legal system: criminal law and civil law. A civil lawsuit is a dispute between two parties (a person or a company) that get the court to decide on their disagreement.

A memorial stands at the Minamata Disease Municipal Museum in honor of the thousands of people who died after consuming seafood contaminated with deadly mercury wastes.

Two photos from Minamata, Japan, taken in 1993. Top: Demonstrators march in support of legal action against the company accused of dumping industrial toxins that caused Minamata disease. Bottom: People suffering from the debilitating neuromuscular disorder enjoy a cherry blossom tour in Minamata.

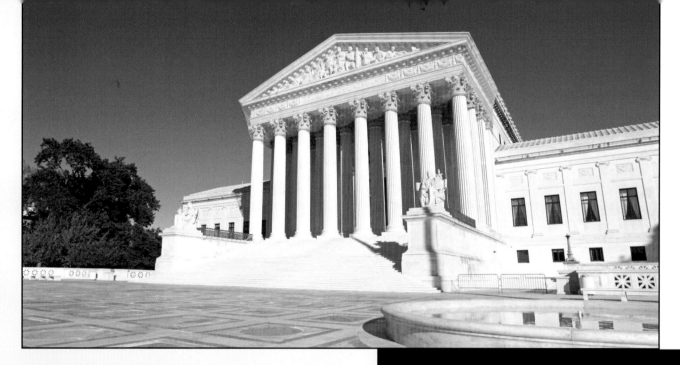

Their argument might be about owing money or who owns property. People don't go to jail if they lose civil lawsuits.

Criminal cases deal with certain kinds of actions, such as murder or assault, that can harm others. In criminal cases, the state (the government) starts the lawsuit and acts as the prosecutor against the person or corporation (called the defendant) who is accused of the crime. The state is called "The People" in the United States and "The Crown" in Canada and the UK.

Don't Make Earth the Victim

People used to believe that polluting was a crime with no victim, and companies usually got off by paying relatively modest fines. That began to change when, in the 1980s, environmental groups started prosecuting company presidents and other decision makers. They wanted the executives to understand that they were responsible for their decisions and could go to jail.

A portrait of the members of the U.S. Supreme Court, taken in 2010: Back row (left to right): Sonia Sotomayor, Stephen G. Breyer, Samuel A. Alito, and Elena Kagan. Front row (left to right): Clarence Thomas, Antonin Scalia, Chief Justice John G. Roberts, Anthony Kennedy, and Ruth Bader Ginsburg.

A SPECIAL CLASS OF LAWSUIT;
A SPECIAL CLASS OF MOVIE

A special type of lawsuit is the class action. A class action lawsuit is a civil action filed by a single person or a small group of people acting on behalf of a larger group. Class action lawsuits often involve injuries or illness caused by a product, such as a kind of medication. They may also involve harm by a company or some other group causing pollution to the environment.

One of the most famous class action lawsuits was the one that became the basis for the 2000 movie *Erin Brockovich*. In that movie, Julia Roberts starred in the title role. Erin Brockovich was the law clerk and environmental activist who, despite her own lack of any formal legal education, led a group of citizens of Hinkely, California, in suing the Pacific Gas & Electric Company for contaminating groundwater with chemicals. The case was settled in 1996 for $333 million. The movie garnered Roberts an Academy Award for Best Actress. Since the movie's release, Brockovich has become something of an environmental superstar herself. She runs her own environmental consulting company, has starred in her own reality-based TV shows, and has participated in several more environmental class action lawsuits.

Today most people recognize that harming the environment is a severe crime—as much so as theft or even, in some cases, murder.

In 1981, the EPA set up the Office of Criminal Enforcement (OCE) so they would have a team of investigators to gather evidence to prosecute environmental criminals. Now OCE investigators work with the FBI and other federal agencies. Like other police officers, they learn special skills at law enforcement training centers.

Healing the Planet

Today, there are much harsher fines for breaking environmental laws.

Erin Brockovich, president of Brockovich Researching & Consulting, testifies before a U.S. Senate committee hearing on Disease Clusters and Environmental Health in March 2011. Joining her is 21-year-old Trevor Schaefer, a brain cancer survivor and founder of Trevor's Trek Foundation, a group that seeks to raise awareness of childhood cancer. Brockovich and Schaefer testified in support of a bill that would help protect children and communities potentially affected by medical conditions that arise in unusually large groups of people. Such conditions may have environmental causes.

Mr. Trevor Schaefer,
Youth Ambassador; and Founder

Ms. Erin Brock
President, Brockovich R
Consulting

Special agents working for the EPA's Office of
Criminal Enforcement collect evidence and
help prosecute violators of environmental laws.

This money often goes to restoring the
environment back to its original state. Even if
the damage is an accident, such as an oil spill,
the company is expected to pay for the cleanup.
If companies see that it will be expensive to
break the law, and that other companies have
to pay fines, then they will get the message—
comply or suffer the consequences.

Money from environmental fines can be used
to improve the environment in other places.
The Environmental Damages Fund in Canada
has collected millions of dollars in fines from
polluters who were fined in court. The federal
government offers this money to environmental
projects across the country. In the United States,
the U.S. Coast Guard's National Pollution
Funds Center offers money to pay for a quick-
response team to clean up the spill and offer
compensation to those people affected by the
damage. Then the center goes after the original
polluters for the money.

A command center in the aftermath of the 2010 BP oil disaster in the Gulf of Mexico. Here BP employees work with members of the U.S. Coast Guard and state and local agencies to coordinate the cleanup effort. The day before this photo was taken on June 17, 2010, BP reported that it would finance a $20 billion fund to compensate people whose jobs and incomes were affected by the spill. Also announced: BP's making arrangements to finance the cleanup effort.

THE POLLUTER PAYS PRINCIPLE

Making polluters responsible for the damage they cause to the environment is an idea recognized by international legal authorities. The practice is called the Polluter Pays Principle (PPP), or Extended Polluter Responsibility.

The PPP means exactly what it says: The industries that cause environmental damage such as oil spills or other contamination must pay for the prevention, control, and cleanup.

The PPP was one of the recommendations from the United Nations Conference on Environment and Development, held in 1992. Officials from 178 countries got together at the conference, also called the Rio Earth Summit, held in Brazil.

Alternatives to Going to Court

Alternative Dispute Resolution (ADR) is a way to settle disputes without going to court. ADR is more concerned with finding the right solution for both sides than with winning or losing.

There are different types of ADR, including negotiation, mediation, and arbitration. Let's say you had a fight with your brother over his new laptop computer. Maybe you borrowed it and then lost or broke it. You don't have a lot of money in the bank to pay him back. Here are three ways to settle things that don't involve going to court:

Negotiation. The two of you sit down and figure out a way to replace the computer. You could offer to pay for a new one out of your allowance over time, or you might give him something of equal value that you own.

Mediation. You both complain to your older sister. She keeps you from arguing, and the three of you work out a solution together.

Arbitration. You are pretty angry with each other, so you won't be able to talk calmly. You ask your mother to make the judgment. She might give you a punishment (no TV for a month for being careless with your brother's possessions) and then demand restitution (paying back) by taking away your allowance until the computer is paid off. Or she might decide that restitution without any further penalty should settle things. In arbitration, you and your brother have already agreed to go along with whatever your mother says.

Any of those methods can be less expensive than going to court. These choices are less about fighting over who wins and who loses and more about finding a solution.

PRECAUTIONARY PRINCIPLE

A precaution is an action you take to prevent harm. Fastening a seat belt in a car or slapping on sunscreen before you go outside in the summer are two examples of precautions. In environmental law, the precautionary principle means the government has a duty to prevent harm, even when the impact of our actions on a complex ecosystem isn't fully understood. This idea offers a reason to create tougher laws rather than wait until all the disastrous effects of climate change or pollution are known.

Members of a U.S. Coast Guard cutter crew remove an oil-covered boom from the ocean on May 8, 2010, in the Gulf of Mexico. The boom was part of a skimming vessel used to remove oil from the water's surface. This cleanup effort was coordinated by the Coast Guard during the BP oil disaster following the April 20, 2010, explosion of an offshore drilling rig operated by BP. In addition to coordinating the cleanup effort, the Coast Guard helped draw BP into the partnership of the military, local residents, and other federal agencies in preventing the spread of oil.

IN SETTLED LAWSUIT, OIL GIANT FINED FOR DUCK DEATHS

In 2010, Canadian oil company Syncrude was fined $3 million for causing the death of 1,600 ducks that it allowed to land on its ponds full of toxic materials. This was the largest fine for an environmental offense in Canada. The company faced provincial and federal charges, and the fine came about as part of an agreed-upon settlement between the company and prosecutors.

Waste material left after the processing of oil creates the kind of toxic-laden pond that killed 1,600 ducks in the Syncrude oil case. The Syncrude oil processing plant is visible in the background.

If you are the peacemaker in your family or you like being a peer counselor at school, then maybe you would make a good mediator.

You Can Be Part of the Solution

Enforcing the laws that already exist to protect the environment can be very satisfying. Like a traffic cop, you are making sure that everyone pays attention to the rules of the road, and you can save lives as well. Bringing lawbreakers

to justice can be a very long process even when you choose to settle the issue outside of court.

A Green Career Path

Today more than ever, we are living in a society in which the word "green" means more than the color of a crayon. As our appreciation for, understanding of, and need to address "green" issues increases, so will the need for people to work in environmental jobs.

CHANGING BUSINESS PRACTICES: ENVIRONMENTAL NON-GOVERNMENTAL ORGANIZATION CAMPAIGNER

We work with hundreds of companies in the book, newspaper, magazine, and print industries to phase out the use of endangered forests and toxic bleaches in papermaking. We also work to make more environmental solutions available and reduce overall paper consumption. Canopy is the organization best known for "greening" the *Harry Potter* books, where 24 publishers of the incredibly popular series switched to ecological paper.

I have always been interested in environmental and social justice issues. I studied environmental issues for both my undergraduate and master's degrees. Since then, I have been active in campaigning for forest protection as well as other environmental issues, including marine protection.

The best thing about my job is that it draws needed attention to the forests that I love—including temperate rain forests on British Columbia's west coast or northern Canada's boreal forest.

If we all valued the natural world around us and were more considerate of our impact on the planet, maybe my job wouldn't be necessary.

Follow your passion, and if that involves advocating for the environment, go for it!

Tara Sawatsky
Corporate campaigner
Canopy
Vancouver, British Columbia

Activists from several international NGOs set adrift large floats in Jakarta, Indonesia, bearing photographs of leaders from the United States, Europe, and Asia. During this demonstration, held in 2009, activists pressed the president of Indonesia, the largest nation in Southeast Asia, to address climate change in meetings with other heads of state.

NATURAL RESOURCES DEFENSE COUNCIL

Even after environmental laws are passed, that doesn't always mean the regulations will be enforced. Sometimes it takes another group to start legal action to get things moving.

Founded in 1970 by a group of concerned law students and lawyers involved in environmental issues, the New York City-based Natural Resources Defense Council (NRDC) has won some major victories in the courts against polluters. The environmental-action organization has also been involved in pushing for stronger environmental laws. After Hurricane Katrina hit New Orleans and the U.S. Gulf Coast, the NRDC tested contaminated soil and urged the government to adopt better cleanup methods. Today, the 1.3 million-member NRDC has more than 350 lawyers, scientists, and policy experts working in the United States and China.

According to the Environmental Careers Organization, Canada has more than 680,000 environmental employees. In the United States, the numbers are even greater. As older people retire in the next ten years, there will be an increasing demand for new employees.

With a background in law, you can explore a variety of careers that will give you a chance to help both people *and* the environment. Whether you plan to work for a government agency, an eNGO, or a law firm—or perhaps teach people to work in environmental law—you will be able to devote yourself to ideals such as clean air and water, and you will make a difference!

A coal-fueled power plant is seen belching smoke from across a field of wildflowers. This view underscores the importance of figuring out ways to be sure that nature can live in harmony with our industrial needs. One way of doing this is by proposing, passing, and enforcing tough, effective environmental laws.

START YOUR GREEN FUTURE NOW...

It's exciting to have plans and dreams for the future. It's also exciting to try new things. While you wait for school to be over, here are some fun projects to help you find out what you enjoy doing and to whet your appetite for your future career.

READ ALL ABOUT IT!

Stay up-to-date on the issues in your community by reading the newspaper or signing up for enviro-newsletters online. That way, you'll know what's happening in time to make your opinion known. Write a comment to the newspaper or newsletter about what you think.

START A GROUP

As any member of an environmental non-governmental organization (eNGO) knows, groups can achieve more ambitious goals than just one person alone. Your class is a readymade group. Ask your teacher about performing an environmental study or holding a cleanup day. You can start a petition to solve a local litter, pollution, or cleanup problem or ask your elected official some questions about government policy.

JOIN A SUPPORT ORGANIZATION

Stay informed by joining a non-governmental organization such as the global World Wildlife Fund (WWF), the Canadian Parks and Recreation Association, or, in the United States, the National Parks Conservation Association. National parks often have community support groups, too. Many towns and cities have environmental associations. They'd appreciate your support and interest, and you would learn more about the activities, mission, and involvement of NGOs in environmental issues.

VOLUNTEER FOR A GREENER FUTURE

Are there parks in your area? You could volunteer as a naturalist and tell groups of visitors about the plants and animals they could see. Annual events such as Earth Day offer a chance to volunteer with a local group. You can also go online and find out more about Earth Day and its founding as a mass teach-in by U.S. Senator Gaylord Nelson in 1970.

ADVOCATE FOR YOUR FEATHERED FRIENDS

The environment is as close as your back yard, and helping its ecosystems thrive can take many forms. Hang up a bird feeder and watch the different species visit your garden. Every December the Audubon Society runs a Christmas Bird Count with volunteers from all over North America. Find out which clubs in your area are coordinating the count, and phone in the number of birds you find in your area. You'll be gathering valuable research!

BE SMART, BE SAFE!

Please get permission from the adult who cares for you before making trips to new places or volunteering in your free time. Always let him or her know where you are going and who you are meeting. If you are getting paid for any kind of work, check the laws where you live to make sure you are old enough to have a part-time job.

GET YOUR FAMILY TO GO GREEN

Become the enviro-enforcer in your family. Issue tickets for breaking the rules: not putting things in the recycling bin, forgetting to turn off lights, or letting the dryer run too long. But don't forget to praise them with positive actions, too. Hand out healthy treats for good behavior!

GLOSSARY

appeal To apply to a higher court to hear legal arguments in the hopes of reversing a lower court's decision. The Supreme Court is the highest court of appeals.

arbitration An agreement to have a dispute settled by a third person

boom A floating barrier used to contain an oil spill

BP A multinational oil and gas company headquartered in London, UK. Its name is derived from *British Petroleum,* the official name of one of the founding companies of BP. On April 20, 2010, the offshore oil drilling rig *Deepwater Horizon,* operated on behalf of BP in the Gulf of Mexico, exploded, killing 11 workers and creating a partially uncapped well about one mile (1.6 km) below the ocean's surface. The gusher from that well resulted in the worst environmental disaster in U.S. history.

carbon dioxide (CO_2) A greenhouse gas that can, when present at certain levels, pollute Earth's atmosphere and other resources and cause harm to plant and animal life

climate change Long-term change in the climate of the planet, usually attributable to human causes. The term is often used to mean global warming.

conservation Protecting plants and animals and their natural habitats

contaminate To make impure by adding a poisonous or polluting substance

criminology The study of criminal behavior

deterrent Something that discourages people from acting in a certain way

dispute A disagreement

ecosystem A complete community of living organisms and their non-living surroundings

emissions Substances (gases and particles) discharged into the air

endangered Species that are so rare they could be wiped out if not protected

extinct No longer in existence

forensics The science of gathering evidence for legal purposes

fossil fuels Fuel sources that started as microorganisms buried deep beneath Earth's surface that were eventually converted to oil, coal, or gas

global warming The gradual increase in temperatures that our planet is experiencing, usually considered an effect of climate change

greenhouse gases Gases created by the burning of fossil fuels. Carbon dioxide (CO_2), nitrous oxide, and methane are all greenhouse gases. These gases are causing the Sun's heat to become trapped in Earth's atmosphere—just as the glass of a greenhouse in a garden center traps heat—and are causing climate change.

groundwater Water found underground in cracks and spaces in rock, sand, and soil. It moves slowly through (or is stored in) layers of rock, sand, and soil called aquifers.

hazardous Dangerous. **Hazardous waste** is waste that is dangerous or potentially harmful to human health or the environment.

landfill A place to dispose of trash and other refuse; a dump. Landfills may be lined with heavy plastic material to prevent contaminants from seeping into soil and groundwater. The waste materials are usually covered with soil and are often used as a way of creating or extending land use.

mediation A process in which two people who have a dispute bring in a third person to help settle the argument

negotiation A dialogue between two people to reach an agreement

neuromuscular Relating to nerves and muscles

pollution Any substance that damages or poisons the air, water, or land. Chemicals spilled into a river, dust from a construction project in the air, or garbage left on a beach are all forms of pollution.

smog (smoke + fog) Visible air pollution that forms a brownish-yellow haze

Supreme Court The highest court in the land. In the United States and Canada, the Supreme Court is the last court to which an appeal of previous courts' rulings may be taken.

sustainable Able to go on into the future; sustainable resources, such as plants, algae, wind, water, and the Sun, can be used with little or no long-term effect on the environment

testify To make a statement (in court)

threatened Species that are in danger of becoming rare in any part of their territory

toxic Poisonous. A **toxicologist** is a scientist who specializes in poisonous substances. **Toxic waste** is poisonous waste material.

tribunal A person or persons with the authority to judge (often part of the administrative justice system)

wetland Having to do with wetlands, which are the natural habitats of rivers, ponds, lakes, and marshes. Wetlands are home to fish, water insects and animals, and waterfowl.

FURTHER INFORMATION

www.vermontlaw.edu/Career_Paths.htm
Looking for more information on career paths? Take a look at the Vermont Law School site. It offers a lot of good advice on environmental law jobs.

www.ec.gc.ca/education/
If you live in Canada, there are many opportunities to volunteer with Environment Canada in your community as part of the Great Backyard Bird Count, Frog Watch, and other programs.

www.fws.gov/volunteers/
If you are in the United States, the U.S. Fish and Wildlife Service offers plenty of opportunities to get involved as a volunteer. Check out the great video introducing you to this agency and its mission and the types of wildlife you can help.

www.davidsuzuki.org/what-you-can-do/
For some inspiration on small things you can do to change the way you treat the environment, check out the videos on the David Suzuki Foundation Web site.

www.earthday.org/
Calculate your own environmental footprint using the Earth Day Network calculator, and keep track of news about the environment.

www.worldwildlife.org/home-full2.html
Read about the success stories on saving tigers and elephants through the World Wildlife Fund's Web site.

www.sierraclub.org/
www.sierraclub.ca/
The Sierra Club runs hikes and other adventure opportunities in both the United States and Canada.

www.gp.org/index.php
greenparty.ca/issues
www.greens.org/
Green Parties all over the world support the idea of protecting the environment. Find out where the closest branch is to you.

www.unep.org/
The United Nations Environment Programme assists countries all over the world on ways to protect the planet.

www.eco.ca/
The Environmental Careers Organization (in Canada) has a great overview of the types of jobs you can look for in the field.

www.epa.gov/climatechange/kids/index.html
The U.S. Environmental Protection Agency has a kids' Web site where you can learn more about climate change as well as tips on green living.

INDEX

INDEX

ABOUT THE AUTHOR

Susan Brophy Down is a newspaper journalist. She was the enviro-enforcer in her family, convincing them to eat healthy food and recycle. She used to live in a log cabin on the west coast, and she likes to hike, sail, and go bird-watching.